Some praise from readers

# SWAMI HARI

I am a simple forest monk

---

"We read special books like this every morning after breakfast together so that we can savour them. You've done a wonderful job putting the book together."

— Drs. Martin and Marian Jerry, Authors of *Sutras of the Inner Teacher: The Yoga of the Centre of Consciousness*

"I began reading it as soon as I opened it up. I've ended up reading the book twice, it's quite inspirational."

— Santosh Jagadeeshan, Ph.D.
Panama City, Panama

"Adjectives I would use to describe this book are: beautiful, magnificent, warm, sentimental, golden..... and that is my favorite word, it's an absolute golden treasure."

— Jyoti Bratz, The Yoga Society of Milwaukee

"Thanks for sharing with us the truly wonderful life about this remarkable, wise and humble saint from the Himalayas. It makes one want to catch the next plane out to Tarkeshwar."

— Howard Judt, First initiate of Swami Rama in the United States. Past president of the Himalayan International Institute of Yoga Science and Philosophy

"I was deeply touched while reading. Very inspiring. You have captured the spririt of Swami-ji in this book."

— Jagdish Thakoerdin,
Amsterdam, Netherlands

# SWAMI HARI

I am a simple forest monk

# SWAMI HARI

I am a simple forest monk

Daniel Hertz

SWAMI HARI: I am a simple forest monk

© 2009, 2010 (Second Edition) by Daniel Hertz.
All rights reserved. No part of this book may be reproduced or redistributed in any form or by any electronic or mechanical means, including information storage and retrieval systems, without the prior permission in writing of the copyright owner.

Daniel Hertz
Email: SimpleForestMonk@gmail.com

ISBN: 978-1456505875

Cover design and typesetting:
Jay Larson *www.jaylarsondesign.com*

*This book is dedicated to those poor Himalayan communities that through countless generations have produced great Yogis who have journeyed out into the world and shared their wisdom for our benefit.*

## Only Breath
—RUMI

Not Christian or Jew or Muslim, not Hindu, Buddhist, Sufi, or Zen.

Not any religion or cultural system.

I am not from the East or the West, not out of the ocean or up from the ground, not natural or ethereal, not composed of elements at all.

I do not exist, am not an entity in this world or the next, did not descend from Adam and Eve or any origin story.

My place is placeless, a trace of the traceless. Neither body or soul.

I belong to the beloved, have seen the two worlds as one and that one call to and know,

first, last, outer, inner, only that breath breathing human being.

*…Swami Hari carried a copy of this poem in his wallet…*

# Contents

**Foreward** — i

**Preface** — 1

**Essays**
Swami Hari — 7
At One with Nature — 24
There is Always Room — 30
The Real Yes Man — 35
Staying Positive — 46
Sleep and Death — 52
To Be — 58
Living with Aging — 65

**Poems**
Swami Hari — 71
Peace — 72
Look for Me — 73

**Excerpts from Lectures**
What is Love? — 75
The Truth is Hiding within You — 77
I am a Simple Forest Monk — 78

**Notes** — 79

**Words of Thanks** — 83

**SRIVERM** — 85

# Foreward

## The Himalayan Sage Swami Hari

Rare and fateful are those moments in one's lifetime, when one comes into direct contact with a personality that indelibly changes the course of one's life. The Himalayan sage Swami Hariharananda, affectionately known as "Swami Hari" was one of such personalities in the early days of the 21st century.

He was a direct disciple of the legendary Swami Rama of the Himalayas. For twelve years he lived, took care of and rebuilt the ancient Tarkeshwar Temple in the Himalayas, a place where his Master Swami Rama attained enlightenment. Tarkeshwar is one of the most special pilgrimage places for the worshipers of Lord Shiva. Here, Swami Hari lived and worshipped alone for many years and witnessed many miracles brought about by his 'grandfather' – as he liked to call Lord Shiva.

Soon after his Master Swami Rama left his body in 1996, Swami Hari left Tarkeshwar: first, to visit all the yoga and meditation centers that Swami Rama had founded in the United States since 1969; and second, to continue the work of Swami Rama and the Lineage of the Himalayan Masters.

Swami Hari's first visit to the United States in 1999, his teachings, travels around the country to come in touch with old students of Swami Rama, and his subsequent annual visits to America are the subject of the new book by Daniel Hertz, *Swami Hari: I am a simple Forest Monk*.

It is a collection of essays about the life, work, and teachings of Swami Hari during his visits to the United

States between 1999 and 2006. Interesting photographs, several poems and brief excerpts from Swami Hari's lectures give the reader additional insights into the personality of this 'simple forest monk', as he liked to call himself. But his students and friends knew better. Swami Hari was an example of a modern-day sage, accomplished spiritual guide, and devoted disciple of his Master. He appeared suddenly – as if from nowhere, and a few years later his health deteriorated to such a degree that he could no longer travel. Yet, during the few years that he traveled around the United States, he got to meet many spiritual students and seekers, mainly through the grace of Swami Rama's leading disciple, Swami Veda. It was Swami Veda, who made the necessary introductions in the beginning, and gave him much support through the Meditation Center in Minneapolis and other yoga and meditation groups that he had founded across the United States and around the world.

But teaching and giving special guided meditations which enabled one to greatly deepen one's meditation practice were not all that Swami Hari accomplished. As students would give him love offerings, he used the money to start a technical and vocational school in the Himalayas. The place selected for it was in the town of Malethi, located near Swami Rama's birthplace in Toli. Starting with nothing, by the time Swami Hari left his body in June, 2008, several buildings of the school complex were up and running, and had 90 students enrolled in one of four programs: electrical work, plumbing, computer programing and operation, and tailoring and sewing. New initiatives are being developed now, including the cultivation of herbs and roses. In these remote Himalayan places, these educational opportunities are of the greatest value to the young people: they give them a chance to learn a useful trade, and then be able to make a living in their home area, instead of moving away to a large city in search of work.

The book describes all of this and more. Those who knew Swami Hari will at once recognize his modest, cheerful and loving personality through the words of the author. The words and thoughts contained in this remarkable book will bring into their hearts the fond memories of Swami Hari and his life and work – both dedicated to serve his Master and to help others.

Consul B. John Zavrel
Clarence, New York
August 2, 2010

## Foreward

## Simple Forest Monk

What a creative and constructive river of love and wisdom Daniel has permitted to kindly flow through his mind and heart to his pen (or shall we say computer cursor and keys). Thus this simple and sweet book of reminiscences and reflections now becomes a perennial stream for the love and wisdom that crystallized for a few years in the name and form of Sri Swami Hariharananda Bharati to continue to course through the currents of our embodied lives and water afresh the dry and parched places of our minds and hearts.

First meeting Daniel over a decade ago at our Guru Deva Swami Rama's Ashram, Sadhana Mandir, in Rishikesh where Swami Hari was then dwelling as a respite from the austere life at our beloved Tarakeshwar Ashram, in the higher reaches of the Himalayan hills, we played like happy cats to serve and love Swami Hari to help, according to our small visions, make his life more comfortable and pleasant there. Swami Hari's surrendering nature to prakriti's whims made those pastimes quite easy and sweet. Daniel, do you remember the time, while Swami Hari was out, perhaps for a lugubrious stroll at the banks of the Ganges, we gathered up all his possessions and bedding and moved his place up to the more spacious and sunny and airy room he then occupied overlooking the Ganga 'till his departure from this mortal plane. In his simplicity and humbleness, Swamiji would never have efforted himself for a change of venue from the colder, darker room. Swamiji accepted this sudden change in fortune, as he did the myriad and sometimes fantastic episodes of his life, with a simple "O.K, Baba." Knowing full well, it was not his life he was leading, but rather a life lived as the silent witness of the grander lila, the awesome play of the divine. And seeing this life lived this way, was one of the most grand and appreciated teachings of our beloved Sri Swami Hariharananda Bharati. Oh, Baba, we know and feel in our hearts that your life and love affirming laughter has survived the funeral pyre, and continues to echo gently as we pursue our lives left on this terrestrial plane ephemeral.

Jai Guru Deva Maharaj Ki Jai!

In the Love and Light of the Saints and Sages of the High Himalayas,


Ma Sewa Bharati
Rishikesh, India
June 15, 2010

## Preface

Dear Reader,

   Swami Hari made many friends over the 10 years that he traveled around the world. These were his "brothers" and "sisters" as he liked to call them. But even though in that time he became very worldly, he never lost his child-like wonder about the world. Like a child, his laugh came easily and naturally and was very infectious. He could never quite believe that a poor forest monk from the Himalayas who had been living in isolation for many years had somehow become a world traveler. The only way he could understand it was to give all the credit to his Guru, Swami Rama. He would say, "Oh, Baba," and laugh as he shook his head. He tried to teach all of us how to laugh and shake our heads as we go through life, even if things don't always go exactly as planned.

   During the 5 years that we spent most of our time together, we were almost inseparable. I am not sure why he kept me around so much, but we did laugh a lot when we were together. I helped him where I could, but I didn't know how to make Chai (tea), which he loved, or Kitchari, which he ate a lot of when he was having digestion problems. The one time I tried to make Kitchari (a one-pot traditional Himalayan Mountain dish) for him, the rice was not cooked enough, but he was polite and said, "That's fine, I'll cook it in my stomach." Eventually he taught me how to cook Kitchari, and shortly after that it became a mainstay of my diet.

   The last talk he gave in the U.S. was in the fall of 2006 at the Institute for Health and Healing at Abbott-Northwestern Hospital in Minneapolis, MN. His last words in that talk were, "I'll be back." He said it 3 times in a row and I am not sure what he meant by it, but I do know that he is back in the minds and hearts of many of the people who met him. The last time I talked to him was by phone in February of 2008. We called India to see how he was doing and he was staying at the SRIVERM project in Malethi. His last words to me were, "I'm in trouble." I took this to mean that he knew his condition was worsening rapidly and there was nothing that could be done to help him. He ended up passing away several months later, in June of 2008, at the Himalayan Institute Hospital Trust in Jolly Grant, India. He was cremated on the grounds of a temple he built called the Tangleshwar Mahadev Temple. It is located near Malethi at the confluence of the Madhu Ganga and Nayar Rivers.

A couple of months before Swami Hari passed away, I was inspired to start writing about him. I don't know where the inspiration came from, but it was a very strong feeling coming from deep inside of me. The words needed to come out and be expressed. The first essay I finished was the one called "Swami Hari." I sent it to India and he was able to read it before passing on. At that time he gave me his permission to publish the writings. I continued working on the essays over the next year. At the time my wife and I were living in Panama. Panama has a very suitable environment for the growing of vegetation and somehow it was also fertile ground for writing.

Swami Hari's major goal during those ten years of travel was to raise enough money to build the project that he called SRIVERM (Swami Rama Institute of Vocational Education and Research Malethi). He said that the building of the project was fulfilling instructions that Swami Rama gave to him many years before. All of us who met him were also beneficiaries of that project, for during that time he had to travel to raise the funds, we received many teachings from him. By the time he passed away, SRIVERM was up and running. As stated on the project's website in July, 2009, "SRIVERM continues to be a source of hope for remote mountain villagers. The Malethi Elementary School currently has 87 students in grades K-6. The vocational school has 90 students enrolled in one of four certified programs: electrical work, plumbing, computer programming and operation, and tailoring and sewing. There have been 128 vocational graduates so far. And there are new initiatives being developed, such as the Rose Cultivation Project. As of 2009 over 8,000 rose plants are under cultivation for the production of rose oil." There is an exciting 2010 update. The SRIVERM Bachelor of Education College has been granted certification seats for 100 Himalayan Mountain villagers.

There are two purposes in mind for this book:

1. To continue to raise funds for the SRIVERM project

2. To introduce people to Swami Hari who did not have a chance to meet him in person

I hope you enjoy it.


Hari OM,


Daniel Hertz

# ESSAYS

# Swami Hari

"I am a simple forest monk."
—SWAMI HARI

I met Swami Hariharananda Bharati on my first trip to India 10 years ago, in November of 1998. The day after I arrived in Rishikesh to study Yoga, I took a walk along the Ganges River, near the ashram where I was staying. A woman swami, Ma Sewa, approached me and asked if I was the Yoga teacher from Minneapolis. I was surprised by the directness of her question and how she would have known that about me. She told me that a Mountain Yogi had just come down to the ashram because of health problems. She went on to say that she was setting up a Yoga Therapy program for him and asked me if I could help. She had a strict daily schedule of three sessions a day arranged for him that included a walk along the river, gentle stretches, and guided relaxations before each meal.

She wanted to get started right away, so she brought me up to his room to introduce me. She told him I was a single, 41 year old Yoga teacher from the United States and that we would start on the Yoga class routine the next morning. We were to meet in the upstairs Meditation Room at 7:00 AM. He looked from me to her in a gentle, quizzical way that seemed to say, "What am I getting myself into?" Before we parted, seemingly out of nowhere, Ma Sewa asked him, "What do you think this guy should do, get married or renounce?" Again I was surprised by her directness. He didn't respond to her question and I thought it was because he didn't know enough English to understand what she was saying. Several months later I found out the answer to her question.

The next day we got started and for the most part we followed the routine Ma Sewa had set up for us. Most of the Yoga exercises we did were part of a series of Hatha Yoga exercises referred to as 'Joints and Glands'. We did many of the sessions while sitting in a chair. Swami Hari and I would directly face each other, as if we were looking in a mirror. These exercises are done very slowly with a great emphasis on the breath. They are considered beginning Yoga exercises, but as I discovered while practicing with Swami Hari, they are actually very advanced. They are simple and slow, which allow you to go deep inside when practicing and they become very meditative in nature. The sessions continued, three times a day, for several weeks. The movements kept getting slower and slower until finally one day all I could do was sit in silence, without any movement. To move or to speak seemed disruptive. That is when I realized that for all the time we were doing the exercises, he was teaching me, rather than the other way around. I was becoming his student and was given the opportunity to sit with someone who was teaching me in silence. He spoke very little English at that point, but even if he had, the silence was communicating more.

During the walks we took three times a day along the Ganges, we would occasionally try to talk, but it was difficult because of the language barrier. On one walk, I asked him if we had known each other before this life and he said, "Sometimes a father and sometimes a son." That is all he said on the subject. If questions came into my mind, I would ask him, and many times he would answer, "God knows." This was his favorite expression and he used it quite often. He was always willing to help whenever he could. One time when we were walking I told him that I was having trouble memorizing the Gayatri Mantra. He then began to sing the Gayatri to me in a melody that helped me learn it very quickly. I still remember that tune he taught me and can picture him dancing as he sang it. It reminded me of Tevya from Fiddler on the Roof singing, "If I were a Rich Man."

An early morning walk with Swami Hari, Daniel, and friend along The Ganges, Rishikesh, India 1998.

If he saw someone he knew as we were walking he would be very social and loved to laugh, but after walking for ten or fifteen minutes he would like to sit down on the rocks and face the river. I would join him on a nearby rock and we would stare together at the river and eventually close our eyes and practice meditation.

One day, as we were looking across the river into the forest on the other side, he asked me if the United States looked like this. I told him parts of it are a nature reserve like this and parts are much different. That gave me the first clue that somehow he knew he would be visiting the United States some day.

By that time he had started giving occasional Satsangs, or talks, at the ashram. The first time I saw him give a Satsang something strange happened. I looked at him and saw my uncle, then I blinked and saw my father, and then I blinked again and saw Swami Rama. I told him about it the next day when we were walking and he was very interested. He brought up that incident several times over the years and said that was one of the reasons he felt such a responsibility to me.

One thing he loved to say in the Satsangs was that he didn't know anything. In fact, sometimes he said it so much in the beginning of a talk that people would start to wonder why they had come to listen to him in the first place. In the early Satsangs a common topic for him to talk about was that the Navel Center was the True Center of Knowledge. This always took people by surprise since the Heart Center or the Eyebrow Center was more commonly seen to be the Center of Knowledge.

The best time to ask him a deep question and to get an answer was during or after the Satsang. Somehow he came up with an answer at that time. Many times during the talk, people would ask him questions and that would seem to stimulate something inside of him to keep talking. If someone asked him a question that was difficult, such as the nature of the universe or something like that, he would close his eyes for a short time and then would answer the question. He was very good at answering challenging questions when he was in a meditative state of mind. If someone asked him a deep question at some other time, he tried to answer, but preferred they would ask those types of questions during the Satsang because he said otherwise it disrupted his digestion (perhaps this related to his idea of the Naval Center as the Center of Knowledge).

## Swami Hari: I am a simple forest monk

One of his favorite topics in those early Satsangs was talking about his experiences with the animals in the forest at Tarkeshwar where he had lived. Tarkeshwar is a holy forest ashram in the Himalayas where he had spent the previous 12 years in intensive meditation practice. He loved to talk about the lions, tigers, crows, monkeys, bears, and cobras. For the fun of it, one time during a Satsang I asked him who would win in a fight between a bear and a tiger. He answered as if he had witnessed it. He said if a bear could find a tree branch to swing at the tiger, it would win. Another time a person asked him about how the population on the planet was growing if the same souls were being reincarnated. He said that more human souls were coming because so many trees were being cut down. Someone else asked him a personal question about their reincarnation history and he said it was better to come into the present moment and not to dwell on the past.

He said he didn't plan his talks ahead of time and didn't know what was going to come out of his mouth, but that he enjoyed listening like the rest of us. He also used to love to talk about what Tarkeshwar was like when he first arrived there. Years before, when he first decided to go live at Tarkeshwar, many people would stop him on the road and ask why he was walking there. They told him nothing was there anymore and the previous "Baba" of the ashram had passed away. He said all he found when he arrived there was an old shed and a fire pit with a broken tea cup. He decided to sleep there that first night and in the middle of the night he woke up and felt a body lying next to him. He recognized it as the spirit of the previous Baba and that spirit implored him to develop Takeshwar into a full ashram as they had discussed in detail many years before. He was able to accomplish all that and more in his time there.

But most of all, he loved to talk about his beloved master, Swami Rama of the Himalayas. His grandmother and Swami Rama's mother were sisters, so after Swami Hari's family had to leave Pakistan during the partition of 1948, they settled in Swami Rama's hometown of Toli (a three hour walk through the hilly forest from Tarkeshwar). Swami Hari was a young teenager by this time. Swami Rama was 15 years older and had already left Toli by the time Swami Hari arrived. Swami Hari (not yet called that) pursued Swami Rama for the next 35 years, requesting to be initiated as a swami and was turned down by him nine times over that period. Swami Rama sent him away each time without granting his wish, sometimes even refusing to see him at all. Then one day Swami Rama came in the middle of the night, with no notice, to visit him at Tarkeshwar to initiate him as a monk in the Himalayan Tradition. He told him his initiation would be the next day. Swami Hari had already been a monk for almost 20 years, since he was 36, but said he only felt like a real monk after the initiation with Swami Rama. He didn't like to talk about his past, the time in his life before he became a monk, and these details came out slowly over time.

For the next several weeks we continued the Yoga Therapy routine that Ma Sewa had set up and he eventually asked me when I was going to visit Tarkeshwar. It was located about 100 kilometers north of where we were staying in Rishikesh. We planned a trip up there for one night, on New Year's Eve. He came along so he could drop off some supplies for the workers there and to pay their wages. Because of the cold weather and his health problems, the altitude made it difficult for him to stay there for longer than the one night. But at least I got to see it and could now understand a bit better about the experiences he had there. It was quite clear that he was really in his element when he was there. I noticed that

## 13   Swami Hari: I am a simple forest monk

something came over him as he walked down the path and entered the great forest. He seemed to gradually go into an altered state and was at the peak of his spiritual

Tarkeshwar.

power as he became in perfect harmony with nature once again. His will seemed to become nature's will. The night we arrived he chanted around the campfire so joyously that it was almost like a baby returning to its mother after a long separation. Tarkeshwar is located in a beautiful old growth forest with very tall fir trees and was at about 6500 ft. elevation. It was a simple ashram with several rooms for guests. There was no electricity or plumbing and they cooked the meals over a wood fire. There was also a very old Holy Temple there which was considered to be highly charged with meditative energy. The whole forest area actually felt this way. It is something that you could sense in a subtle, yet clear way, as you entered the main gate. Swami Hari had renovated the buildings of the Temple over the years, but he kept the sacred ceremonial pieces inside. Villagers told me that these holy Shiva Lingam stones had been there for at least several hundred years.

After our return from Tarkeshwar, we again continued with the Yoga sessions and walks until my departure from India. At the end of my three month stay in India, we parted ways, not knowing if we would see each other again. In February I returned to Minneapolis, but the memories of my trip to India stayed with me. Much to my surprise, a few months later, in May, a wealthy member of the Yoga tradition sponsored a trip for him to the United States. The plan was for Swami Hari to stay at that person's house, about an hour outside of Minneapolis, for several months in the summer of 1999. Swami Hari was not well known at that time, but because he was one of only a handful of direct disciple monks initiated by Swami Rama, people were curious to meet him. The director of the Meditation Center in Minneapolis scheduled him for a Satsang (talk). Since I knew him from the previous winter, they called me to ask if I could pick him up at his sponsor's house. When Swami Hari came to the door, the first thing that came out of my mouth was, "I'm going back to India with you." I don't know where that came from and it was totally unplanned, but shortly after that I did request another leave from work and ended up traveling back to India and Tarkeshwar with him in the fall. (It turned out to be good fortune that I traveled with him on that return trip to India. He was not feeling well the whole way back. He simply pulled his wool cap over his eyes and sat up straight in meditation for the whole flight, without talking to anyone. When we arrived at the airport in Delhi he was so dizzy that he had to sit down immediately after we got to the baggage claim and I wheeled him to the waiting taxi. He mentioned several times over the years how grateful he was that I was with him at that time.)

In the car ride to the Meditation Center he asked me when I was getting married. I was taken by surprise and didn't know what to say, but it did answer the question Ma Sewa had asked him the first time we had met—should this guy renounce or marry?

In the car he also talked about how he could not believe that a poor, simple forest monk from the Himalayas was giving a talk in English in the United States. It was beyond his wildest dreams to think something like this was about to happen. He could not believe how different his life was now compared to how he was living just several months before. He started out that talk with a big laugh and kept laughing continuously for the next minute, non-stop.

There was a crowd of about 25 people and everyone in the room felt the child-like joy and pure innocence emanating from him. It turned out that this talk was the first of many talks he gave that summer in the Twin Cities and beyond. He learned more English as time went on and he eventually became quite fluent. Over the years he liked to tell the story that for his first lecture at the Meditation Center he only knew three words in English: "yes," "no," and "maybe," and that he still couldn't figure out how the words for the talk came out.

After that first Satsang, he soon moved into the Meditation Center. The demands for his time grew as more people heard of him and heard him talk. In the little spare time he had he loved to watch Swami Rama videos. He would watch them over and over again to learn what he was saying, and also to practice his English. He also loved to walk from the Meditation Center to the banks of the Mississippi and sit and chat with anybody from the

Center who had walked with him. Whenever I would say, "It is a beautiful day," he would always, without fail, correct me and say, "Everyday is a beautiful day." He said this no matter how cold or rainy or humid or hot the weather was. He also said it no matter how sore he was from all the dental appointments he had.

Swami Hari and Daniel at the Meditation Center in Minneapolis, Minnesota, 2001.

That first summer he had major dental work and was in pain for much of the time. He couldn't eat much then because his teeth hurt. He was offered a lot of nice food from visitors, especially the Indian families, but felt bad that he couldn't eat it, so to be polite he would often eat and simply bear the pain. On later trips, when his teeth felt better, he developed some digestion problems from all the travel, so he still couldn't enjoy the nice food that was offered to him. He laughed a lot about the irony of that.

He also laughed a lot about the time he applied for a Visa to Taiwan and several weeks went by without him receiving his passport back that he had mailed in. He needed his passport for a flight that was approaching soon, so someone advised him to go to the police as soon as possible to ask for advice. This turned out to not be good advice. We took him to the downtown Minneapolis police station at midnight and the police were busy with prostitutes, robbers, etc. While we were waiting for the police to talk to us, Swami Hari saw the posters of the Most Wanted criminals. When the police finally talked to us, they thought we were crazy when we asked them about the Visa problem and sent us home. After that he jokingly referred to himself as the Number One Most Wanted Swami. His passport came back without incident shortly after that.

He was surprisingly knowledgeable about current events and business, and had a good intuitive sense about what was happening in the world. Long before the stock market tumbled when the technology bubble burst in 2000, he told me to sell off all my stocks. To my great loss, I declined to follow his advice at the time because I figured he was a forest monk and couldn't possibly know anything about stocks.

In the beginning, while his health was better, he also liked to go sightseeing. One time I took him to the top of the Foshay Tower (34 stories) in downtown Minneapolis where there was a lookout on the top floor. We saw a film about Foshay, the man who built the tower, and he was sure that he was some famous Guru in a previous life. He had a love of mechanics and building, so when I took him on a boat ride through the lock and dam system on the Mississippi River he was very interested. We even went to a Minnesota Twins baseball game when they still played in the domed stadium. He had never seen an indoor stadium, and the size of it (seating 60,000 people) shocked him. He enjoyed the game, even though he didn't completely understand the rules. To add to the experience, the people behind us spilled beer on the floor, which he totally ignored.

Another time we drove to Chicago to see the Glenview Branch of the Himalayan Institute. He said that Swami Rama had instructed him to see all of the Centers he had established in the U.S., and since Glenview was being sold, he told me he had to see it. We arrived unannounced and Swami Hari waited in the car while I went inside. I told the secretary that there was a monk from the Himalayas in the car who was a grand nephew of Swami Rama. She was in disbelief until I brought him in to see for herself. Eventually the director there agreed to let him stay in Swami Rama's former cottage for the weekend. When I went to pick him up at the end of the weekend he was very grateful for the experience. He told me that even though there were plenty of mosquitoes there to bother him, he had the deepest 24 hours of meditation he had ever had.

Daniel, Eric Ness, Ma Sewa, and Swami Hari on a trip to Daniel's cabin in northern Minnesota.

We had a chance on all the trips and sightseeing to talk a lot, and whenever we did, he remained persistent in his assertion that I needed to get married. He was puzzled that with all the single women in the world, it had never happened before this. Because both of my parents were deceased and we had become very close, he felt it was his obligation to help me accomplish this task. I think this was the cultural norm in India, but in the United States it was unusual to have an advocate like this. No matter what we did, it was an ongoing topic of conversation between us. Each summer when he visited he told me it would be, "The summer of marriage." Eventually it did happen. In the summer of 2003 I met Nikki at the Meditation Center. Almost immediately after I met her, Swami Hari told her she should marry me. It took a special woman not to turn around and run away after that. To my good fortune, things worked out, and she became my life partner. The card he gave us at our wedding said, "My long project is now complete." At the age of 47, I was married for the first time. But as it turned out, he was also in the process of finishing other projects which now had his complete attention.

He commented several times over the years that while traveling he was never able to duplicate the deepest states of meditation that he could reach at Tarkeshwar. The students who loved to meditate with him in his morning sessions would probably not agree with that, since many commented on how deep they could go with his guidance. He established a rapport with adults and children very easily, made many friends, and his joyous energy drew many people to his talks. Many people started to come to him for help and advice, and he was always happy to meet with them. As he became more fluent in English each year, he covered a much wider range of topics in his Satsangs. He still loved to talk about Swami Rama, but also shared more information on his practices and his interpretation of classic Yoga texts. For someone who claimed to be uneducated, he had sure done a lot of reading in his life. Throughout it all, he would emphasize that Yoga was a science, not a religion. He felt that assigning a baby a religion when they were born caused much divisiveness in the world. It caused people to focus on how they were different rather than what they had in common. Another theme that ran through all his talks was the importance of cultivating a positive state of mind while meditating. To help accomplish this, he said that each morning, at the first awareness of wakeful consciousness, it was important to smile. It was a way of showing gratitude for living another day.

Swami Hari, with Nikki and Daniel at their home in South Minneapolis, 2004.

That first trip to the United States turned out to be the first of eight years of summer visits that he made. Each summer that he returned he would expand the number of cities that he visited, but would always include Minneapolis/St. Paul as his longest stop. He visited many more places in the United States (north, south, east, and west) and eventually many places in the Caribbean, Europe, and Asia. He gradually became a comfortable world traveler and learned his way around the airports. Each year more and more people invited him to come and visit their Yoga centers and he accepted all the invitations. Wherever he went people were so happy to see him that they gave him unsolicited donations. He used the money to give something back to the Himalayan Mountain community where he was raised. He said he was acting on instructions from his Guru, Swami Rama, and he focused his unbending determination on reaching these goals. He was an experienced builder and used the initial money to build a computer school in Toli, India, Swami Rama's home village.

The money kept coming and he eventually started to build a huge, poly-technical school in Malethi, India (one hour drive from Toli) which he called SRIVERM (Swami Rama Institute of Vocational Education & Research, Malethi). I was told this school is the biggest building ever built in the Himalayas. It is in a beautiful valley and the Tarkeshwar ashram location can be seen in the distance. The institute serves the people of the poor mountain communities who had little access to quality education and training before that. This is a multi-million dollar undertaking that is still in process. Even though his health deteriorated more and more each year, he would not let go of the goal of building SRIVERM. It opened for classes in 2005 and served over one hundred students at that time, with room for many more. In one section there is a program for small children who are starting their school careers, and the education program now continues to serve the students as they move through the grades. In another section there is a program where young adults can receive vocational training in areas such as plumbing, electicity, and computers.

When I visited SRIVERM in 2006, I finally started to

understand his vision for the project and what a great thing he had done. It gave the people in that area the most important thing he could have given them: hope for the future. There are also many other plans in the works. He continued to work on that project until his last breath.

SRIVERM Inaugural Ceremony, Malethi, India, 2005. From left to right: Dr. Rajiv Uttam, Ma Devi, Vijay Dhasmana, Dr. Mittal, Swami Hari, V.P. Singh, Swami Jaidev, Swami Ananda Bharati, and Dr. Vinod Upadhyay.

Little did I know when I went to India that first time that I would meet someone like Swami Hari. In fact, I had no idea that a person like him even existed in the world. He showed me, by example, how much one person could do to make the world a better place and what a one-pointed mind could accomplish. I am grateful to have been a witness to the process. What is around the next corner? Swami Hari told me that Swami Rama asked him one time if they had known each other before, in a previous life. At first Swami Hari didn't know what to say, then all of a sudden the thought came rushing into his mind and he answered, "Yes, we have known each other for many births." Swami Rama replied, "Well, this should be your last." I asked Swami Hari what he would do after this life if he wasn't reborn, and it was no surprise when he

23   Swami Hari: I am a simple forest monk

replied, "God Knows."

# At One with Nature

"Life is like a river."
—SWAMI HARI

Above all else, Swami Hari's philosophy was based on nature. Nature itself was the miracle for him and it acted as his guide. He was, simply and clearly, a man of nature. He felt that nature, with all its imperfections, is somehow perfect. He knew life from what he felt in his bones, not from what he read in a book. This knowledge came from the deep meditation disciplines that he practiced in the Himalayan forest ashram of Tarkeshwar, where he lived in near isolation for over 12 years. Any person who has practiced meditation over a long period of time can appreciate the courage and discipline it takes to undertake such a great physical and emotional challenge. The Catholic monk, Thomas Merton, described it like this in a 1964 essay called *Rain and the Rhinoceros*: "The man who dares to be alone can come to see that the nothingness which the collective mind fears and condemns is a necessary condition for the encounters with truth. It is in the desert of loneliness and emptiness that the fear of death and the need for self-affirmation are seen to be illusory. The solitary, far from enclosing himself in himself, becomes every man. He dwells in the solitude, the poverty, the indigence of every man."

His normal schedule during those years of isolation was to go to bed early, at about 8:00 PM. He trained himself to awaken automatically at midnight and he would sit in meditation until 6:00 AM. He preferred to eat just before going to bed, otherwise he said he would get hungry while sitting in the night. During the day he managed the affairs of the ashram and had tea with the occasional visitors who wandered through to meet him and feel the strong spiritual vibrations of the area. There is some kind of magnetic energy permeating the Tarkeshwar valley that is clearly noticed by many of the visitors. If they don't notice it when they arrive or while they are there, they feel some definite change after leaving the area.

Entrance to Tarkeshwar.

He was all about something very primitive, more about the hills and rocks that are billions of years old. If anyone could discover the secret of life, you'd think it would have been him, but even he couldn't run away from death. After many years of struggling with emphysema, he passed on in the summer of 2008. He didn't talk about it much, but his lung capacity was about 35% in the first year he visited the U.S. (1999), and by the eighth and final year the capacity had dropped to around 25%. Donald Culross Peattie, a government botanist and freelance writer, wrote in 1935 that, "The courageous thinker must look the inimical aspects of his environment in the face, and accept the stern fact that the universe is hostile and deathy to him save for a very narrow zone where it permits him, for a few eons, to exist."

Swami Hari did exist, and it was in perfect harmony with the natural rhythms and cycles. This was most apparent when I observed him in Tarkeshwar. He was clearly in his element there. Tarkeshwar is described as an unusually sacred and holy place in *Living with the Himalayan Masters* by Swami Rama. After being gone for 6 months on his first trip to the United States, in 1999, I had the opportunity to see Swami Hari at the moment he arrived back at Tarkeshwar. I observed him transform before my eyes as he walked down the path from the parking lot to the ashram. He walked slowly, taking in all the sights and sounds around him until he gradually became one with his surroundings. It was as if he walked together with his teacher, nature herself, until they were in perfect harmony. I am not sure what came first: his thoughts became nature or nature became his thoughts. Sigurd Olsen, the prominent naturalist from Minnesota, wrote, "when one becomes completely immersed in the ancient rhythms, then one begins to live."

Tarkeshwar is believed by many to be the home of Lord Shiva, one of the major Hindu gods. In his early Satsangs in the United States, Swami Hari often talked about his relationship with Shiva. In a spiritual sense, he related that at first they were at odds, but eventually Swami Hari

27  Swami Hari: I am a simple forest monk

Swami Hari calling the crows in the morning at Tarkeshwar.

came to see him as his kind and gentle grandfather. He shared how he "talked" to him in the way a child talks to his grandfather. He would have these special talks when he needed something special for the ashram or for others who needed his help. His early Satsangs also covered topics such as his experiences with the various animals who lived in the same forest as he did. These included crows, monkeys, cobras, lions, tigers, and bears. He also loved to talk about how he came to Tarkeshwar and his relationship with the previous Tarkeshwar Baba. Many years before he actually lived there, Swami Hari would visit that previous Baba now and then and discuss plans for how Tarkeshwar could be improved in the future. Several years after that Baba passed away, Swami Hari wandered to Tarkeshwar and found only an old shack and a broken tea cup. Over the years he followed the plans set out by that previous Baba and today Tarkeshwar is a beautiful ashram and temple.

In the Satsangs he would often give simple meditation instructions, such as, "Thoughts are like cars, you want to increase the space between them." Another favorite topic in those early Satsangs was how "$1 + 1 = 0$." I think what he meant was that when one human is joined to Atman (the single, unitary divinity), he becomes 0. Enlightenment to him was about becoming less, not more. Swami Hari also loved to refer to the spiritual superhighway comprised of the billions of living things (humans, animals, plants, and insects) that are constantly dying and being born. This process, at first glance, seems mysterious to people because it seems so hidden. Lewis Thomas won the National Book Award in 1974 for his book of essays called *The Lives of a Cell: Notes of a Biology Watcher*. One of the essays is called "Death in the Open". In it he writes that, "Everything in the world dies, but we only know about it as a kind of abstraction. Almost everything you can catch sight of is in the process of dying, and most things will be dead long before you are. If not for the constant renewal and replacement going on, the whole place would turn to stone and sand under your feet."

The Shiva temple at Tarkeshwar.

Swami Hari was most known for his laugh. It was infectious. When he entered a room, you could feel a positive surge of joy. Being in his presence could somehow relieve all the worries of life that we carry around. When he passed away in the summer of 2008, mother nature must have heaved a large sigh, for one of her brothers had moved on. Many of us also noticed a change in our world without him. But Swami Hari was beyond the time and space that most of us identify with. He seemed to live in the eternal, nonhuman time that can only be glimpsed by looking at the vast mountain ranges or ocean depths. There is something about him that seems as if it will live forever. It is almost as if his spirit is flowing in the rivers and his breath is now synchronized with the blowing of the wind. Wendell Berry wrote that, "All wildernesses are one. This fragment of the wilderness is also joined to other times; there flows over it a nonhuman time to be told by the growth and the death of the forest and the wearing of the stream." Swami Hari showed us that many of the answers we seek are hidden in nature, if we can only find a way to see them.

## There is Always Room

"The answers are hiding within you."
—SWAMI HARI

Before I met my wife Nikki, Swami Hariharananda Bharati gave me many encouraging talks about how important it was that I should get married. One time I asked him, "But isn't it important that you be in love with the person?" He shrugged his shoulders and asked, "Love? What has love got to do with it?" At the time I did not understand what he meant, and I still don't think I fully understand it. Perhaps it has something to do with fulfilling our karmic duties. Another guess is that love is always there, you just have to learn to access it. A different way of looking at it that has helped me is that love can grow anywhere if nurtured properly. We love our family, but if our circumstances were somehow different and we had been raised by a different family, we would probably love them also.

Shortly before we were married in 2004, Nikki's mom sent us a copy of Swami Rama's book *Love Whispers*, which she found in a small used book store in northern Idaho. We were excited to see that it was an autographed copy, with Swami Rama's signature inside the front cover. In the book he describes how difficult it is to talk or write about love: "Love is the most ancient traveler. It is beyond human expression, and therefore inexplicable, for you can feel, but not speak about it. There is no word in any language that can convey the true meaning of love." When I started this essay, I knew that it would be very challenging for me to write about the topic of love. I realized that I still had so much to learn. I had a lot more questions than answers.

One time I heard someone say to Swami Hari, "Thanks

from the bottom of my heart." His reply was a question, "Does your heart have a bottom?" To him, the heart was infinite, with no boundaries. I remember him putting these beliefs into practice in different ways. Whenever anyone asked him for a ride, he would not hesitate. The answer would always be if there is enough room in the heart, there is enough room in the car. Whenever anyone was near-by when he was about to eat, Swami Hari would ask them if they were hungry and would like to join in the meal. If they asked if there was enough food, he would say that if there was room in the heart, there was enough food. He always seemed to be open to everyone and anyone joining in, no matter what activity was going on. It was about having an open heart towards people. He expressed often that it was important to bring people together, rather then build walls to separate them. As an example, he felt religion pushed people apart, rather than together. He thought it was a problem that when a baby was born he or she was given a religion and immediately a boundary would go up. It teaches the child that this is for us and that is for them and that makes us different from them. He felt it caused the wars and most of the other problems in the world.

In this same way, Swami Hari thought that the boundaries between countries are a problem. We create boundaries rather than looking at the big picture and calling ourselves citizens of the world. Instead we say we are a citizen of this country or that country, just like we are on a team competing against one another. This separates us as humans and can create great disparity between places. For example, the countries or people who have wealth may not be inclined to help out others, especially if they are from a competing or different country. I have noticed that when the President of the United States ends a speech, he says, "And may God bless America." What about the rest of the humans out there? Perhaps if people realized the common experience we are sharing as humans it would help give us a common bond. Can you imagine what would happen if 2 or 3 humans were transported to another planet, and they were the only humans living there among many other creatures. Wouldn't they naturally feel a love toward each other? If we can somehow realize that this common experience of living as a human being on the same planet at the same time is very special, maybe we will start to treat each other as family, regardless of the different countries or religions that divide us now.

The heart is commonly seen as the organ responsible for many emotions, including love, compassion, and joy. Through the study of Yoga we can look at the heart in both spiritual terms and how it functions biologically. The Anahata Chakra is the key spiritual focus point for many Yoga practices. This chakra is physically positioned in the heart region. When one makes decisions from this chakra, they are said to be made from one's higher self. We have all experienced pain in the heart after a sad event, or an opening of the heart after a joyous response. Everybody talks about love, about how we fall in love, or how we love our children or spouse. But do we really understand what love is? Swami Veda Bharati is considered by many who have met him to be a Yogic Master of the heart chakra. I heard him say once that if someone truly opens his heart chakra, he would be an enlightened being on the same level as Jesus or Buddha. One time in a satsang in Rishikesh, India at the Sadhana Mandir Ashram, a question came into my mind very strongly and I asked Swami Veda, "How can one learn to love others as you do?" He responded without hesitation, "How does a mother learn to love her child?"

Swami Rama used an advanced technique of Yogic Mastery to become the only person ever to demonstrate under laboratory conditions that the heart can be temporarily stopped (or at least slowed down to the point to where medical devices cannot detect it beating). In 1970, almost 40 years ago, he stopped his heart from pumping blood for 17 seconds. Reports of this research have been well documented in numerous scientific publications. What he did was very unusual and dangerous for most of us to try, but we can learn from his experience and apply it to our daily lives. In medical terms, the role of the heart is to pump oxygen-rich blood to every living cell in the body. The human heart beats approximately 80,000 to 100,000 times a day and pumps almost 2,000 gallons of blood. This means that in a person's life lasting 70 to 90 years, the heart beats approximately two to three billion times and pumps 50 to 65 million gallons of blood. Yoga philosophy says that the more you slow your breath, the longer you will live. Through Yogic breathing and relaxation exercises we can see that it is possible to self-regulate the heart rate. In Biofeedback you can connect a sensor to a person and a computer screen will show you the amount of heart beats per minute at any particular time. It shows us that the heart speeds up on the inhalation (sympathetic nervous system) and slows down on the exhalation (parasympathetic nervous system). One simple Yoga breathing exercise that allows us to slow down the heart and learn self-regulation is called two-to-one breathing, which means the exhalation is twice as long as the inhalation.

New research shows that the feeling of love has a biological basis. Researchers have recently found that love works chemically in the brain like a drug addiction and can be isolated to a tiny area of the brain which forms a circuit of love. If the part of the brain that creates the feeling of love can be artificially stimulated, some day we may look at love in a whole new way. But isn't love more than just a chemical reaction that can be quantified and researched? Not everything can be measured. In his book *Love Whispers*, Swami Rama wrote that, "When this life ends, the mystery of love begins." If this is truly the case, how can we even imagine what love means when we are in this life?

# The Real Yes Man

> "...because until you are completely non-violent you cannot understand truth."
> —SWAMI HARI

While on a short break from our life in Panama, my wife Nikki and I went to visit relatives in Los Angeles for a couple of days over the winter holidays. We had some free time and decided to see a movie. I was attracted to a movie called *Yes Man*, starring Jim Carrey. It was playing close to where we were staying and the start time was convenient. But most of all, the title reminded me of Swami Hariharananda Bharati, a Himalayan Mountain Yogi who I had met in India ten years ago. Swami Hari's background was obviously much different than the character in the movie, but he was a living model of what it takes to put the philosophy introduced in the movie into practice. The movie was about a bank loan officer who said no to all requests for loans. This negative approach carried over into the rest of his life. He refused to accept invitations to any sort of social engagements that his dwindling supply of friends offered. He was stuck in this pattern and it was unattractive to others, including his ex-wife who he still longed to be with. One day an old friend ran into him and somehow convinced him to attend a motivational seminar. At the seminar he is confronted by the speaker and agreed in front of the whole group to say yes to everything that is asked of him for the next year. It was difficult at first, but he tried it and one thing led to another. He eventually got a promotion at work, met an attractive lady, and experienced many new things. His life became fun for him to live and fun for the audience to watch.

Swami Hari and Daniel in Duluth, MN, 2001.

Swami Hari at Minnehaha Falls, Mineapolis, MN, 1999.

37   Swami Hari: I am a simple forest monk

Swami Hariharananda Bharati, 2003.

Swami Hariharananda Bharati, 2003.

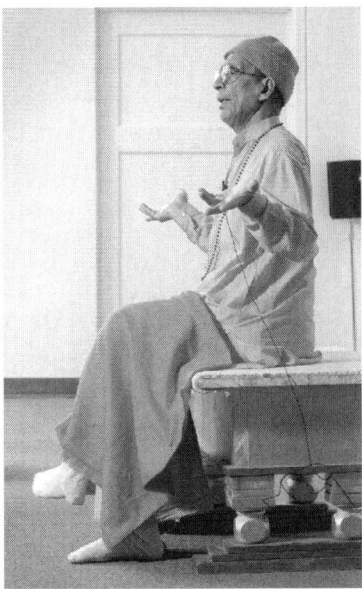

39   Swami Hari: I am a simple forest monk

Swami Hariharananda Bharati, 2003.

Over the years I had a lot of opportunities to observe Swami Hari in India and on his visits to the United States. It became very clear to me that the word "no" was not in his vocabulary. At first it was hard to believe and I couldn't understand it, but eventually I saw the wisdom in it. Mostly he said "yes" whenever he was asked to do something such as go on a trip, or to someone's house, or to give a lecture, or to see a movie. He believed things happen for a reason, and to him every request was an opportunity to take another step towards completion of his goal of building a huge educational project in the Himalayas. When it seemed like he wanted to say no, he still did not say it. In those cases he would say something like this out loud, "Oh, Baba," and then typically close his eyes while he contemplated what to do. When he closed his eyes like this he was consulting with his Guru, Swami Rama. He did this often because he felt that everything he did was in the service of his Guru. He said many times that his mission was to fulfill the instructions Swami Rama had given him many years ago. I don't ever recall him saying he would do something for himself. The words me, mine, my, or I were not in his vocabulary. Sometimes he would agree to do things and I could not figure out why, but he would be content with his decision. I asked him often why he said yes to that person or accepted an invitation that didn't make sense to me. He told me several times that he was like a dry leaf being blown about by the wind. On his first visit to the United States, we took a walk by the Mississippi River in the fall, and I saw a lot of dry leaves blowing around. I pointed to the leaves and asked him if he noticed what I did. He nodded and smiled.

Eventually I realized that his approach of saying yes was directly a result of taking his vows of renunciation. When he took his vow to become a monk (or swami or sanyasin) he surrendered everything he owned in the world, including his home and all personal preferences and desires. The idea is that the whole world then becomes your new home. You even renounce your own religion, and therefore become part of all religions. By taking that vow, he gave up all remaining desires for sex, family, wealth, comfort, fame, and reputation.

Swami Hari addressing a group of school children at Dudarkhal Intermediate College, near Toli, India.

*The Bhagavad Gita*, a sacred Sanskrit Hindu scripture, defines it as performing actions without seeking the fruits of the actions. It means not owning any possessions, and only using what you are given. Taking the vow is not like turning on a switch and all of a sudden you lose your desire for all these things. For the most part, it is only making official what has already happened through years of intensive meditation practice. He talked many times about feeling like the King of the Universe when in a deep meditation, no matter how "poor" he was at the time. To reach and maintain this level requires an absolute surrender to the universe, a tremendous amount of courage, a steel-minded resolve, and an unshakeable faith that if you are not given something, then you don't need it. All this is done with the aim of attaining the highest goal. Some people describe this goal as enlightenment and others define it as self-realization. Whatever you call it, everything is done with the intention of service to humanity. The process of renunciation is considered the same as if you have died. Even in the present civic law of India, renunciation is considered death. It is one thing to take a vow, and another thing to put those vows into practice. Living his life as a Yes-man allowed him to fulfill his vows. How was he able to say yes to so many things and still remain content with his decisions? My best guess is that once death is experienced, what else is there to lose?

The life of a renunciate is obviously not for everyone, but I think that is what it takes to carry out the Yes-man philosophy in its truest and purest sense. Most of us don't have the inclination or fortitude, but Swami Hari took that philosophy to the extreme by fully surrendering to the forces of the universe in his initiation into Swamihood. A person can be harshly tested if they carry out the vows of renunciation to the fullest degree. Many difficult challenges and obstacles can be encountered. He called himself a dry leaf, being blown about in the wind. Dry leaves can fly in the breeze, but they can also be stepped on and crushed. I remember telling Swami Hari about a frog I had observed at my cabin and he was very interested in hearing the story. In the summer, many frogs climb up the porch screen to be closer to the porch light that I keep on all night. Out of all the frogs who did this, I found only one who climbed up to the window on the 2nd floor to be closer to the light up there. When I told him this part, he nodded, as if he was thinking that yes, there is always someone who goes against the crowd and climbs to a higher level. He paused to contemplate what this frog did and seemed to identify with it. Then I told him that when I went to close the upstairs window late at night because

43   Swami Hari: I am a simple forest monk

From left to right: Randall Krause, Swami Hari, and Claudia Crawford, Dr. Uppreti (far right), and various ashram staff and guests.

it was chilly, I heard a crunch in the hinge of the window. He grimaced and guessed what I was going to say next. It was the spine of the frog that was caught in the window. It was still alive when I finally saw it, but breathing with great difficulty. I felt terrible about it and wanted to do something to help it. I released it from the hinge and placed it onto the roof. It stopped breathing shortly after that. Swami Hari nodded at the end of the story as if he felt a lot of empathy with the frog. He knew that when you surrender it all and stick your neck out above the crowd, sometimes you can get hurt. The forces of intensive spiritual energy, both positive and negative, swirl around you. But that did not stop him from his practice or his mission. He seemed to sense that it came with the territory.

Swami Hari discussing plans for further development of the SRIVERM project at the SRIVERM campus, Malethi, India, 2006. In center, Rodney Huff and Michael Gormley from Minneapolis, MInnesota, USA.

At the end of the movie *Yes Man*, the lead character learns that he has to balance his approach so he can function appropriately in the world (and stay out of jail). He realizes this philosophy has to be put into practice in a moderate way. The whole idea is to open up to people and opportunities and ideas that come your way. But good judgment and common sense have to be applied to it. He continues to take the path of saying yes, but finds out it is OK to say no if it is morally or ethically wrong or if it hurts himself or others. Another key point is that his job and life remained constant. He did not have to quit his job or find a new apartment. The only variable was his new attitude of changing his reaction to the events that crossed his path. His new way of reacting put everything in a different light. Saying no then became a conscious choice rather than an automatic reaction. When I met Swami Hari, I found someone who lived his life as a Yes-man. Becoming a monk is not something that all of us believe in or have as a goal, but the approach of saying yes more often can be put into practice by all of us. The result can be a whole new way of looking at life and what it has to offer.

## Staying Positive

"If it happens, good. If it doesn't, double good."
—SWAMI HARI

Are you looking for a challenging practice in addition to the standard Yogic practices of fasting, silence, and sleeplessness? The practice of "staying positive" can be a lifetime practice in the same way that meditation or Yoga is. It is so easy to fall into the negative way of looking at yourself and others. We are presented with many things in life that could very easily cause us to become cynical or pessimistic. We have all come face to face with the death of a loved one, a diagnosis of a serious illness, a violation of our personal property or space, discrimination based on our religion or the color of our skin, an unexpected job loss, or any other of the infinite possible scenarios that humans commonly encounter. At first glance, these things are horrible and seemingly happen for no reason at all. In the middle of writing this essay, for example, the apartment that Nikki and I moved into four nights ago in Panama City, Panama was broken into while we were sleeping and Nikki's laptop computer was taken along with my wallet. I felt awful about it since we had not taken all of the security measures that we could have. Looking at it in hindsight allowed me to see where we made our mistakes. But dwelling on the mistakes caused me to slip into a more negative stream of thoughts. I decided to attempt to put into practice what I was writing about. It was not easy and every now and then I found myself getting angry about what happened. But when I really thought about it, I realized all the things we have to be thankful for. First of all, we were not physically harmed, which has to be the most important thing. Second, most of what we lost is replaceable (except Nikki's research on

## 47   Swami Hari: I am a simple forest monk

the computer that was not backed up). Also, because of the incident, we have become more aware of security in general while in the apartment and around town. Perhaps because of that we have averted some incident that could have happened in the future that would have been worse. We never know why things happen, and that is where having faith that things happen for a reason is really tested. It is that kind of faith that we rely on to support us in the process of staying positive.

Swami Hari, Swami Veda, and Pandit Dabral, three great Yogis and three great teachers in the same tradition.

Something Swami Hariharananda Bharati, a Himalayan forest monk, once said to me comes barreling into my mind now and then—"Wake up with a smile on your face." He not only said it, but I saw him put it into practice many times over the years. Whenever I saw him first thing in the morning, he would always greet me with a smile. It is such a simple and effective practice, but it can also be very challenging at times. The simple act of smiling can change the outlook for the day. To smile means there is something positive in the approach to the day. No matter how hard things seem at the time, a smile can remind you that there is a lot to be thankful for. A smile, in a small way, acknowledges that there is something to be positive about even if it seems hidden away somewhere. I never asked Swami Hari directly how he stays so happy all the time, but by observing him over many years, I noticed a very distinct philosophy that he had. He was never disappointed if things didn't go the way he wanted them to go. He planned many projects in great detail, but was not attached to the results. He would frequently say, "If it happens, good. If it doesn't, double good." What I think he meant is that there is something good to come out of it either way, if only we can learn to accept the result of our actions. This is part of the process of surrendering and having full faith that things happen for a reason, whether we understand it or not. Swami Hari was a master at this approach, probably perfected over the many years of his intense meditation practice deep in the forests of the Himalayas. But he strongly believed that everyone has the potential to learn what he did if we practiced enough and had the proper guidance.

This practice of being positive requires constant attention. There is so much negativity in the world. We don't even have to leave home to experience it. We only have to turn on the TV or radio news, read the newspaper, or talk on the phone to a friend or family member. It takes a real keen awareness not to fall into a negative way of thinking since the negative approach is so prevalent in many (not all) of the places we go, and many (not all) of the people we come in contact with. Every action we experience can cause negative or positive thought patterns. It depends on how we interpret the events around us. This does not mean to walk around in a bubble and ignore or be blind to negative things we hear or see. It means to acknowledge them and feel compassion, but not to make it the central and dominating theme in our lives. Like it or not, the people and places we surround ourselves with can influence us. If we are aware of this influence, we can learn to be positive all over again. It is habit forming, one way or the other. To break a deep and prevalent habit is not easy, that is why staying positive is a lifetime practice. It has to be cultivated. It is like hitting a baseball. Out of every ten thoughts that come into the mind, if three of the ten are positive, that is a pretty good average. To help bring our thoughts to the positive side, we have to plant seeds and create a fertile environment. Eventually more and more of our thoughts will lead us to the doorway of gratitude, love, compassion, giving, and joy. Until that time comes, every thought or interaction with others is challenging us to find the positive.

Nikki and I have been living in Panama for three months so far and have about nine more months to go to complete our planned stay of one year. Sometimes I find it very easy to think about all the things I don't have here- long-time friends, easy access to quality, organic food, a house like we had in Minneapolis, efficient means of transportation, and quality health care practitioners that I know. I could easily allow myself to wallow in those thoughts and whine to my wife that I don't like it here. But then, somehow, something wells up inside of me and reminds me- it is not about what we don't have, it is about what we do have. If I allow myself to see it, I have so much to be positive about- time to explore writing, reading, and the study of Spanish, good health, clean water and plentiful supply of food, a suitable place to live, easy access to the internet, a nice and loving wife, and purposeful work activities. The list could go on and on in either direction, positive or negative, and I have come to realize that it is my choice on where I focus my attention.

Satsang with Swami Hari.

At the very core, focusing on the negative comes from worrying about something in the future that has not happened yet, or replaying in our mind something that has already happened. When this happens, it is important to remind ourselves that what happened in the past is over and that we don't know what the future will bring. If we can somehow come to that realization, it can release us from the bonds of expectations and bring us more into the moment. Being more in the moment leads to a more positive state of mind.

We are tested almost every step of the way in life, sometimes brutally, as we attempt to develop a more positive approach. Sometimes it just seems easier to complain like everyone else does. It is not easy to be content with what we are given. We are presented with many things in life that seem like we have no choice in what they are. We are born into some family, in a particular country, and at a specific time. We can be grateful for the things we are given or the opportunities we have, or we can wish that we had something else. Wishing that we have something else is a sure path toward focusing on the negative. When we are grateful for what we have, it is positive. Have you ever met someone who is a positive and happy person, no matter what is thrown at them in life? This type of person is rare, but they are so inspirational and such a bright light for all of us to learn from. Swami Hari strongly believed that all of us have the potential to be that person.

# Sleep and Death

"When spirituality and science meet...that will be a great day..."
—SWAMI HARI

Sleep is as common to humans as the sun or water. It is essential and we need it every day. Without it we would perish. With it we can live. But what about the ultimate form of sleep? Death is the sleep in which we say farewell to our bodies. It is the sleep in which our bodies do not wake up. Death and sleep are linked together in a way that is not understood well. There is good reason for that. Death is seen as a morbid topic that people like to ignore if possible. But sooner or later, we cannot ignore it. We are all faced with death in one way or another. It catches up with all of us eventually. Death can be an uplifting topic, depending on how we look at it. Sleep can help us explore the process of death. It can show us how to make the process of dying more familiar and therefore less scary. Fear comes from the unknown. Sleep can give us insight into death and therefore relieve our fears and anxieties about dying.

As we age we look at death differently. As children we don't know what to make of it, even when directly presented with it. As adolescents and young adults we don't think it can happen to us. As we move into middle age and beyond, we start to come face to face with our own mortality. It becomes easier to see that we are vulnerable. The decay of the body is easier to spot. If we live long enough, there will be times in our lives that we have closer encounters with death. And when we do, it hurts, no matter what age we are. We look for comfort in the grief and we look for meaning in the life that has passed on. It can trigger us to look for deeper meaning in our own life. It can cause us to examine what we have done and what we will do in whatever time we have left. We realize how suddenly it can come and how fast our lives pass by. We start to wonder what type of legacy we are leaving behind. Is the legacy through our work, our family, or through other contributions to the overall good of society? We ask ourselves what is really important and what does this mean for how we spend our time. It can cause our values and priorities to shift. Sometimes we radically change our life in response to encountering the death of a loved one. We change jobs, move out to the country, or adopt a more positive attitude. Whatever our response, a lot of times it is short lived. We make changes, adjust to those changes, and then the thought of death goes on the back burner. When the grieving process is finished, we fall back into the pattern of going through our lives and not thinking about death until something forces us to all over again.

Roughly two million Americans die "anticipated" deaths each year. These people know they are going to die because of a diagnosis of some kind. That is enough to get most people's attention. Some still don't believe they are going to die, even after hearing a fatal diagnosis. But whether we believe it is going to happen as anticipated or not, it is still going to happen sometime. It is the only fact we are certain of from the moment we take a birth. It cannot be negotiated. Some believe when our time is up, it is up, no matter what we do. In Yoga philosophy, the time we have in the body is determined by how you breathe and how often you do it. Others believe we have a say in how long we live based on what we eat, how much we exercise, and what relationships we cultivate. Regardless of which philosophy you follow, the bottom line is the same. We are out of here either way, at one time or another.

Let's face it. We are mixed up about death. There are many unexplained gaps in the process. The unexplained gaps widen when it comes to quantifying what actually happens at the moment a person leaves their body. Dr. James Hallenbeck, an associate professor at the Stanford University School of Medicine, who specializes in care for the terminally ill, says the vast majority of people go into some kind of altered state as they are leaving their body. Hallenbeck considers this altered state to be a hallmark of dying. The cause of the altered state is due to an intense shifting of our focus and concentration inward. As the body deteriorates, we lose our frame of reference and are forced to pay more attention so we can keep track of what is happening. It is well documented that people lose their ability to speak in the final moments before leaving the body, so they cannot describe what is happening, even if they knew. What actually happens to our mind is unknown. We can only guess. After someone dies we cannot call them on the phone and ask them what happened. It is clear that most things about a dying person's state of mind must be inferred. Even in a normal, healthy state, we are very limited in our ability to describe our state of mind. Try examining your mind right now and see if you can capture the essence and depth of it. It is very elusive and difficult to precisely put into words.

There are many big questions about the universe that seemingly don't have answers. We can't look up death on the internet and find out what happens to our mind as we leave the body. Science can only take us so far down the path. Many ancient and modern religions have a theory on what happens, but no one can know for sure. Some people claim they have gone through the tunnel, seen the light, and come back again. But how can that ever be substantiated? There is a way, however, to empower ourselves so we can decide for our self. The answers do not lie outside of us. The knowledge is not from an outside source, but from our own experience of sleep. It is right in front of our face, but because it is so simple and obvious, we miss it. It doesn't occur to us that the process we go through when falling asleep can be used to learn about the process of death. We don't need to depend on anyone for answers to the questions of death. Each human being is given the tools to learn about death because every human being falls asleep and wakes up again. We do this many times in our lives, depending on how long we live. We have been given a glorious learning opportunity.

I started looking at death in a different way when I started studying Yoga. I started looking at sleep in a different way while studying Yoga in India several years ago. Swami Hari, a mountain Yogi from the Himalayas, explained to me how he learned Yoga Nidra or Yogic Sleep. Some call it sleepless sleep. It is a technique to move into a deep state of relaxation while maintaining a conscious mind. Your body is in a sleep state but your mind is in a waking state. Many of us have had this experience without even knowing it. Have you ever woken up from a nap and felt your mind awake, but couldn't move your body? Or have you ever dozed in and out of sleep and sometimes caught yourself in an in between state, not sleeping or waking? Another way of thinking about it is with dreams. Have you ever woken up in a dream and been conscious enough to take action and not just be blown about by the winds of your unconscious mind? These experiences are all very similar to Yoga Nidra.

This is how Swami Hari explained the process to me. He said you can learn Yoga Nidra by watching yourself fall asleep. Even though we may have experienced this accidentally, it could take years of practice to learn to do this consciously. If you try it sometime, you realize it takes an unwavering concentration. If you really pay careful attention when you are falling asleep, you will not fall asleep. Your mind is occupied. But if your concentration wavers for a split second, before you realize it, you wake up the next morning and wonder what happened. You can drive yourself crazy with a practice like this if you are not ready for it. It can cause you to lose a lot of sleep along the way. It is best to practice it when you have a lot of free time and can experiment with sleep patterns. One way is to get less sleep at night, so naps are needed during the day. If you are taking several naps each day, it gives

Swami Hari and Pandit Ananta (now Swami Ritavan), "brothers" teaching a Yoga Nidra class together.

you more chances to watch the process of falling asleep. If you are really serious about learning this, it is best to find a qualified teacher. The practice can put your nerves on edge and be very jarring. The preparation work for a practice like this is to become adept at deep relaxations. The steps in learning this type of deep relaxation are outlined by Swami Rama in the book *Path of Fire and Light, Volume II*. It is a relaxation process called Shithali Karana.

Why are we not spending our lives figuring out how to die? Sleep, like death, is the ultimate act of surrender. We let go of all control when we fall asleep. Sleep is an adventure, as if we are entering another world. There is no assurance we will wake up again. Because of this, going to sleep can be a catalyst for bringing us to the edge of life everyday and helping us feel more alive. Swami Hari said to wake up with a smile on your face as a way of giving thanks for the chance at another day. Many things about the process of dying are unknown, but it doesn't have to be. Imagine the burden lifted off us if we could be free of our fears about death. We could live our life freely and to the fullest. If the fear of death could be overcome, we could start truly living. Living in the moment, without being haunted by the ultimate fear. It is all about internal freedom. That exhilarating feeling we get when a great burden is lifted off our shoulders. What is there left to fear if we are not afraid of death? The answer is nothing. Being fearless about death means we have nothing to lose.

## To Be

*"Breath is the bridge between mind and body... those that know the value of breath...know the art of yoga..."*
—SWAMI HARI

Let go. Let go. Slow the breath. Relax. Relax. Focus on the flow. Follow the breath. Release. Let go. Seems like I've been sitting a long time. Check the timer. Only one minute has gone by. Keep with the flow. Let go. My knees are tight. I need to adjust. Sit up straight. Relax the shoulders. When shall I go grocery shopping? Should I bike or drive? I need to walk the dog. I'm a little hungry, is there anything to snack on? Why did she say that to me? Who needs it? Whoops. Daydreaming again. Check the clock. Five minutes is almost up. Ding. OK. That's enough for today.

I remember very clearly the first time I sat down to practice meditation. It seemed like the hardest thing in the world to make it for five minutes. And I emphasize the word 'practice' meditation. What passed for meditation that day was simply sitting in the same spot for the five minute goal. After I finished I opened my eyes and my dog was sitting facing me. When the ding went off he must have opened his eyes at the same time as me. He looked at me in a very curious way, like he was trying to figure out what in the heck I was doing. I started to practice regularly for short periods of time, so the dog got used to me sitting in that same spot in the same way. But no matter how used to it he got, he would still keep a curious eye on me. When I would go to set the timer, he would also take his position and keep me company.

What is the process of learning to meditate? First and foremost it takes some good teaching from some experienced meditators. It is important to find an authentic teacher who has learned the craft from someone in a long tradition where the teachings have been passed on for many generations. Something must be transmitted from teacher to student. I found that I added a new teacher now and then to fit where I was at the time. I would be drawn to someone as a teacher and study with that person in depth for some time. Then somehow I would be filled up (not fed up) from that person and it was time to move on. I would then find myself gravitating toward someone else. Often it was an almost unconscious, intuitive process. It was like each teacher had a piece of the puzzle that I had to solve. We are blessed with many great teachers who can guide us through the ancient wisdom of the sages. But we must also realize that everyone we meet is a teacher. The friends who we confide in, the acquaintances we meet through our community and the workplace, even the seemingly random encounters with "strangers." Will Rodgers said, "A stranger is just a friend I haven't met yet."

Second, it takes something deep down inside of us that draws us to the practice and keeps us there, consistently, day to day, through the highs and lows and thick and thin. The devotion may change as we find deeper meaning in what we are doing. At first we may be drawn to it for practical reasons such as stress management and relaxation. Sometimes I find inspiration in realizing it gives us a common link between people. It crosses the boundaries of space and time and connects us to the past, present and future. I can think of so many people I have met in my life who I became very close with and then never saw them again for a variety of reasons. Sometimes I think of all the people I have met in a class, or from a former neighborhood, or knew as a kid, or went to high school with, or crossed paths with during a trip. I am not in touch with most of these people any longer, but many of the experiences were special. Meditation can be the universal tool which unites us all, regardless of physical separation. It can become the common thread which brings all humans together, regardless of any religious or cultural differences. It emphasizes what we have in common rather than how we are different.

Third, all the technical pieces need to be in place: how to sit, when to sit, where to sit, how to breathe, what to practice. The technical pieces change as our bodies evolve, our knowledge increases, and our lifestyle better fits the practice. My body was in no condition to sit properly when I began to practice. This is where the physical postures of Yoga helped me a lot. There are many gentle exercises I was taught that gradually open up the body. The key is coordinating these exercises with the body and the breath. Awareness of the breath is a key to what differentiates Yoga from other forms of exercise. It is important to not force yourself into anything you are not ready for, physically or emotionally. Simply let it unfold. Anytime I felt overwhelmed by all the complex instruction and the physical and emotional release, I reminded myself: keep it simple and enjoy. These are the times when a regular practice is of great help. It allows us to sit there through the storms, maintain our composure, get back on the bucking bronco and release the effort.

All three of these steps in the process are ongoing and continually evolving: 1. Find a good teacher 2. Find the inspiration 3. Keep it simple and enjoy.

The length of time I was able to sit got steadily longer. But what was I doing when I was sitting? If we can get to the point where we are observing the mind for even a small amount of time, this is a big accomplishment. The idea is to somehow separate ourselves from our self. What does this mean? It means becoming the observer and the participant, instead of only the participant. It is a huge accomplishment to somehow see this. It can change everything. More than that, it does change everything. We can learn to ride the wave of breath like a surfer in the ocean. Sometimes we are pulled along and simply glide into the practice and feel like we could sit forever. Other times it feels like we have to push more, to intensify the effort (in an effortless kind of way). But do not be discouraged. As in other pursuits, there are breakthroughs, plateaus, backward slides, and various other events and stimuli that trigger many ups and downs. But even if we can get to that point where we become the observer, it is still only the start. It is like we have arrived in the correct stadium for the sport, but we still don't have a seat, the game hasn't started yet, and the playing field looks uneven.

Once we find our seat and the game starts, we start to peel off layers of clothing. Not because it is too warm, but because we are letting go. Letting go of anything and everything. Letting go of our worries about the future and anxieties about the past. Letting go of our expectations of our self, and anybody else we know or have known. Letting go of our fears, no matter how scary. Letting go of our attachments and our desires. Letting go does not mean we don't care. It does not mean we are a robot. It does not mean we don't have emotional reactions. It means we have those reactions for the love of them, rather than the slave of them. The playing field begins to even out.

When we think we have let go of everything, in truth we

have only taken off the stocking cap or scarf. When we have taken off all of our clothing and are sitting stark naked, we realize that we have three more trunks of clothing to clear out from under the bed and then the six boxes in the basement. After that we go to the attic and then to our parent's house and clear everything there. We go to our friends, acquaintances, everyone and everything we have ever done in this life. When we are beyond naked and our soul is exposed, we are still only beginning. It is like climbing a ladder, reaching the top of the first floor, and realizing we are climbing a 50 story sky scraper.

How does this process of letting go work? We let go by focusing. Focusing allows us to separate the now from the not now. If we are here, how can we be anywhere else? Anything else is only an illusion. Our mind sharpens and our focus does not suppress or bully, but rather just the opposite. When we are focused on the mantra or the breath or the chakra, it frees up anything there that is ready to arise. We let it arise and go on its way while we continue with the task at hand. We set it free and in the process we become free. We become free to explore our very nature. To explore the roots of our being goes hand-in-hand with exploring the roots of our existence. It give us access to the big issues like birth and death and love.

It is hard to say exactly how the practice of meditation has affected me or how I have changed. In the beginning I was able to notice the changes more. People would comment that I looked different somehow. My face definitely lost a lot of the tension I was carrying. At first, for some time, I was sad. I think this was related to seeing myself more clearly. But once I came to terms with what I saw and the fog lifted a little, my moods moderated quite a bit. I felt happier more of the time, and angry less of the time. I have definitely become much more flexible and much less rigid. Not only more flexible in the physical sense, but also emotionally. This changed the whole way I managed my life. I became more open to new ideas and new ways of doing things. I was able to change directions quicker and do things with less planning. I became more confident in my intuitive sense. I started to face the world with more faith. I started to believe that I was in the right place at the right time, even though I could not understand the reasons.

I needed the help of a lot of people, and there were a lot of ups and downs. Gradually the changes became more and more subtle. It was like looking in the mirror everyday to see if I noticed any differences. I could only see the changes with some perspective. I can see I have aged if I compare myself to a picture taken five years ago. But no matter how long I have practiced, it still feels like I am a beginner. The process begins again at whatever place I may find myself on the continuum. I think somehow we always reach the point which gives us the challenge we need at the time. It is sort of a natural equilibrium.

What recourse do we truly have when the universe slams you down and forces you to cry out, "Why me?" What can we do when the physical world loses it shine and we wonder, "What is the purpose of all this?" How can we express ourselves when we are so awed by nature that we are left speechless? What is left for us when buying things and traveling from here to there does not interest us anymore and we ask, "Is this all there is?" I asked myself this question many times. I didn't have an answer. I would throw my hands up in the air and continue to grunt and groan about the state of the world. I still don't have an answer to that question, but at least I can try this: Enter the stadium, find a seat and enjoy the show. Sit up straight, relax the body, deepen the breath, focus the mind and listen. Listen not to the external, but listen to what is speaking to us from the inside. Be calm, be gentle, be open, be positive, be courageous, be moderate, be sensible, be comfortable, be adventurous, be forgiving of our self and others, be free, be the universe, and then simply 'be'.

# Living with Aging

### Epilogue (Written after the publication of the First Edition of *Swami Hari: I am a simple forest monk*) Daniel Hertz, Summer 2010

Almost 20 years ago I came to the practice of Yoga/Meditation looking for help with stress management and a way to heal my body, but it quickly became a spiritual adventure. A couple of years after taking classes at the Minneapolis Meditation Center I decided to make a short visit to the Himalayan Institute in Honesdale, PA. On the flight there, a woman had a heart attack and died on the plane. We had to make an emergency stop in Milwaukee, and I called the office in Honesdale to tell them I would be late for my taxi pick-up in Scranton. The secretary asked me what happened and when I explained the problem she said that there were several books in the Himalayan Yoga tradition that discussed the Yoga philosophy of death and dying. That was when I connected that the higher purpose of the study of Yoga was to learn about the greatest mystery in life: death. After all these years of study and practice, my fears about leaving the body still linger occasionally. At times the panic of it all wakes me up in the middle of the night and it hits me hard: Life is short, it passes in the blink of an eye, we don't know when we will pass this way again, and I am getting older and closer to death.

These brief flashes of panic have lessened some over the years, but tend to surface when I consciously feel the effects of aging. I am 53 now and have definitely felt a slow deterioration in both the body and mind. It seems to go through levels and plateaus. I go through a period of noticing some change in the body or mind, it steadies out for a while, I somehow adjust to it, and then don't pay as much attention to it anymore. For example, in the last year since writing the First Edition of *Swami Hari: I am a simple forest monk*, I have had, for the first time, a visual migraine, eye floaters, a double hernia operation, and tension headaches, to name a few things. I am really interested in the natural, alternative medicine, and I do what I can to research and deal with each issue. When whatever treatment I have tried is put in place, I find my "new" normal, and learn to live with the changes. I have also noticed that I am less resilient to the stressful demands of life and work. I continue to rely heavily on the practice of Yoga, Meditation, and the Relaxation Model of Biofeedback to help me maintain a balance.

Beyond the physical changes, I can feel changes in my mind. Most of the changes are subtle, but there are definitely more blanks in my thought process. By this I mean occasional trouble recalling names of acquaintances and movies that I haven't seen for a while, grabbing the right word to say when I am in conversation with someone, and now and then forgetting where I put things. When these things happen I remind myself to focus even more and bring more attention to the awareness of my thought processes, and that seems to help.

I started checking out books on memory and aging from the library. These books have puzzles and nutritional tips on keeping the mind sharp. They also recommend keeping active, trying new things, and staying involved in the various activities of life, especially after retirement. Meditation, if done correctly (and not simply sitting there and spacing out), is also a tool for maintaining and focusing the mind. I have read that it can support the process of keeping the mind sharp as it ages. Continuing the Meditation practice as I move through the aging process will allow me to see first-hand if indeed this is the case. One book I found extremely helpful in dealing with the headaches is called *The Migraine Brain* by Carol Bernstein, M.D., copyright 2008. It is really a well-rounded book on overall wellness strategies. The number one thing, though, that all the books recommend, is staying in good physical condition. Staying in good physical condition seems to be the key in maintaining the aging brain.

Another book I looked at again recently is *The Art of Joyful Living* by Swami Rama, where he devotes a whole chapter to Memory (Chapter 5 is called Memory and the Nature of Mind). It gives a technique where you sit in an upright relaxed position like you would for Meditation. You then count up to 100 at one number per second, and then count backwards from 100 back to zero at the same rate. The object is to make it all the way without the thought interruptions. If you do have a thought interruption, note when it happens, continue on, and try to go longer the next time without an interruption. He also recommends going to 1000 and back once you have managed to do the count to 100. I have tried the practice (to 100) and found it to be very helpful.

At times the whole process of getting older seems daunting and overwhelming. Most of us will face bodily deterioration as we age and come closer to death. It takes a lot of courage and faith to get through it. It reminds me of the courage that Swami Hari displayed during his dealings with poor health over the last few years of his life. I saw how his body had deteriorated over the years that I had known him. During the first year or two he could go on long walks without a problem. Gradually over the years he needed oxygen more and more until he was hooked up to it almost all the time. He could no longer go on walks or take part in any physical exertion. But no matter how much his body deteriorated, his mind remained as sharp as ever, and he continued with his work and mission. I was often surprised at how he observed everything and could recall small details very easily. When his health was worsening and the time of his passing was getting closer, he wanted to know that I would be well taken care of after he was gone. He commented to me that he was pleased to see I had found a loving and supportive wife. It is another example of his selflessness. Instead of complaining about his own health, he was concerned about me. One of the last things he said to me was, "You never know what life has in store for you, so it is nice to face it with a partner." He knew that Nikki and I could rely on each other during whatever challenges knock on our door. Having supportive relationships and a strong faith are often cited as keys to healthful living in many of the wellness-type books.

Meaningful relationships, exercising the body and mind, staying involved in new activities, and proper nutrition, can all help a person move gracefully through the aging process. In addition to those things, I am relying on Yoga, Meditation, and Biofeedback to carry me through the remaining portion of my years on the planet. When I am sitting in Meditation practice, many times the most challenging issues I am dealing with will come floating into my thoughts. I have found that even the most potent thoughts eventually dissipate. But in the meantime, when the thoughts are still at their strongest, I stick to the routine of repeating the Mantra, keeping my breath slow and deep, and relaxing the body. When it seems difficult to continue the practice and some self-doubt creeps in, the thought, "You can do it," occasionally pops up to counter it. I don't know where it comes from, but it is incredible when it does, for this determination feels like a gift from the higher power. I love it when this happens because it helps me stay positive. Staying positive allows me to continue to move through the various obstacles in my mind and body that I stumble over as I move through life. I get the feeling that the obstacles and challenges will continue to increase as I grow older, and this strength of determination will be the key to dealing with it. The adventure continues.

# POEMS

## Swami Hari

To choose an austere life with no
expectation of future rewards

To have a vision and keep it when you
have no idea how it will come to fruition

To keep your spirits high in the case of
relentless adversity

To fly against all odds of age and illness
to achieve lofty goals

To live practically in an impractical world

To love others as your own son or daughter

To make something out of nothing at all

## Peace

We have to leave
It is part of the contract
When we buy a ticket
We agree to a round trip
No refunds are allowed
No returns are accepted
It cannot be transferred
What can we do
While we are here
To make the most of our time
We remember where we came from
Lose our fear
Wake up with a smile
Treat others with kindness
Laugh
The train arrives
We hop on board
Without looking back
Peace

## Look for Me

...in the wandering soul of the soft breeze

...in the urgency of the water racing over the falls

...in the elegance of a rainbow arching through the sky

...in the radiant brilliance of the sun peeking over the horizon

...in the free flowing spirit of a soaring hawk

...in the balanced calm of a ripple-free lake

...in the healing rhythm of endless ocean waves

...in the glowing sparks of a roaring campfire

...in the dazzling clarity of a star-filled night

...in the pureness of a freshly fallen snow

...in the innocent pleasure of a heartfelt laugh

...in the awesome splendor of the highest mountain peak

...in the unrelenting strength of a swelling river

...in the unbounded expanse of the open plain

*Excerpts from*
# LECTURES

## What is Love?
### Swami Hariharananda Bharati

If GOD will appear here and say "I am GOD," how will you recognize him? Sometime you will ask [for a] certificate and you will be very much upset, because he has no certificate....We have certificates for dogs, not GOD. Is it not?

If somebody will ask, some children will ask their mom "Mom do you love me?" She will say "Yes, certainly I love you." [And if the child asks] "Please tell me how you love me." She will be in trouble. She will not be in a position to say how she loves. She will only say this "If something happens to you, something happens to me." This much I can say. I don't think that she will be in any position to give a certificate for love, but she loves. My brother and sister, there is no certificate of love. Love is itself a certificate. This comes. This is our being. Love. If we are reading about the love, it means that we are mistaken. That will be our learning and teaching. Let this love [come from within you.]

Today we have created walls. You are Hindu. You are Buddhist. You are Jainist. You are Christian. You are this. You are that... Even today we want to cry but not knowing. We are afraid of what people will say and we cannot cry. Where is love? We want to love someone [but are afraid of] what will people think? What will people say? And we are not in a position to love. We want to laugh, but what will people say? And we cannot laugh. Believe me, we [have] become hypocrites.

First step of Yamas is Ahimsa, non-violence. We are in search of truth. Patajanli says if you are really in search of truth, first learn non-violence. He did not put truth first. He put truth second. He said first learn non-violence. Not hurting, not injuring, not thieving, not harming. I think that this is a simple thing. Not killing, not injuring, not harming, not hurting, When this [non-violence] comes

in us, it is love. What more do you want from love?... Simple thing I am telling you.

# The Truth is Hiding within You
## Swami Hariharananda Bharati

There are many, many books on non-violence, but that book will come from inside of you and that will be your own book. And when this non-violence really starts, you will know, really realize what is truth. If you will go through Patanjali Yoga you will see that in Yamas ... Ahimsa [non-violence] is the first and truth is the second. Truth should be first, but why in second? Because until you are completely non-violent you cannot understand truth. That is why Patanjali put truth in second and when this non-violence and truth will occur in you, will come from inside of you, ... that will become your being....This will not be a 'booky knowledge', this will be your own knowledge.

# I am a Simple Forest Monk
## Swami Hariharananda Bharati

If you ask any monk "Why did you become a monk?" He will say "I want to know the truth. I am in search of truth." Many, many people come to me. I am a forest monk. Many people used to come to me [in the forest]. "Swamiji" they would say.. I would say " Why do you want to disturb me? I am enjoying myself. What do you want?" They said "I also want to search GOD." I said "Is your GOD missing somewhere? GOD is within us." I think [GOD] is not missing anywhere, but we are in search. And we are in search of that we have not lost. Is this not foolishness? I think [it is]. My brother and sister, ...learn to love yourself. The day you will learn this thing, [it will be a great day]. ...If you want to love someone, first love yourself.

Swami Hari: I am a simple forest monk

## Notes

### Only Breath

Jelal Al-Din Rumi, Coleman Barks (translator), *Selected Poems* (London: Penguin Books, 2004), pg 32.

### Preface

Pg. 4

Deodar Grove in Tarkeshwar. Oil on Canvas by Mary Bowman-Cline.

### At One with Nature

Pg. 24

Thomas Merton, *Raids on the Unspeakable* (New York: New Directions, 1966), p.18.

Pg. 26

Donald Culross Peattie, *An Almanac for Moderns* (New York: Putnam's Sons, 1935), p.11.

Pg. 26

Swami Rama, *Living with the Himalayan Masters* (Honesdale, PA: Himalayan Institute Press, 1978), p.313.

Pg. 26

Sigurd F. Olson, *Reflections from the North Country* (New York: Alfred A. Knopf, Inc., 1976), p. 28.

Pg. 28

Lewis Thomas, *The Lives of a Cell: Notes of a Biology Watcher* (New York: Penguin Books, 1978), p.96.

Pg. 29

Wendell Berry, *The Unforseen Wilderness: Kentucky's Red River Gorge* (North Point Press, 1991 ), p.56.

**There is Always Room**

Pg. 30

Swami Rama, *Love Whispers* (Honesdale, PA: Himalayan Institute Press, 1986), p.27.

Pg. 33

Seth Borenstein, *The science of romance: Brains have a love circuit* (http://is.gd/56WRJ) Accessed 2009.

**Sleep and Death**

Pg. 52

Originally published in the *Himalayan Path*, Vol. 8, n. 4 (St. Paul, MN: Yes Publishers, 2008), p.11.

Pg. 54

James L. Hallenbeck, *Palliative Care Perspectives* (New York: Oxford Univeristy Press, 2003), p.145.

Pg. 57

Swami Rama, *Path of Fire and Light: Volume II* (Honesdale, PA: Himalayan Institute Press, 1988), p.186.

**To Be**

Pg. 58

Originally published in the *Himalayan Path*, Vol. 8, n. 2 (St. Paul, MN: Yes Publishers, 2008), p.22.

**Living with Aging**

Pg. 67

Berstein and McArdle, *The Migrain Brain*, (Free Press, 2008).

Pg. 67

Swami Rama, *The Art of Joyful Living*, (Honesdale, PA: Himalayan Institute Press, 1989).

**Look for me**

Pg. 73

Originally published in the *Himalayan Path*, Vol. 6, n. 1 (St. Paul, MN: Yes Publishers, 2006), p.15.

**The Truth is Hiding within You**

Pg. 77

Swami Hari. Oil on Canvas by Mary Bowman-Cline.

**I am a Simple Forest Monk**

Pg. 78

Tarkeshwar. Oil on Canvas by Mary Bowman-Cline.

**To read more about
Swami Hariharananda Bharati see:**

*The Laughing Swami: Teachings of Swami Hariharananda,* compiled by Swami Jaidev and Ma Devi, (Yes International Publishers, St. Paul, MN. 2005).

*Walking with a Himalayan Master: An American's Odyssey* by Justin O'Brien (Swami Jaidev Bharati), (Yes International Publishers, St. Paul, MN, 2005).

## Words of Thanks

Thanks to all the people who have helped and supported Swami Hari and SRIVERM with bottomless love and selfless devotion. Many people around the globe opened their hearts and homes to Swami Hari over the years. It would be impossible to make a list of all those deserving recognition without leaving someone out. To all of you whose names are not mentioned, all I can express is the deepest heartfelt gratitude. Please know that your efforts are much appreciated.

After Swami Hari passed on, the donations to SRIVERM started to dwindle since he was not here to tour around anymore. This book and fundraising project came about as a way to keep the flow of donations coming. It has definitely been a group effort and never would have come to fruition if not for the loving efforts of a lot of people. I am an amateur and naïve in the ways of the publishing world and never imagined that putting together a book and fundraising project would be such a huge task. Writing the essays turned out to be the easy part.

Claudia Crawford was instrumental from start to finish in the fundraising and book project. Ma Sewa and Ginny Lechtenberg gave support and encouragement throughout the process. The YES from Jan and Dave Semling helped move the project from dream stage to getting it done.

Thanks to Nandini Avery, B. John Zavrel, Michael Smith, and Randall Krause for help with the proofreading. Thanks to Jay Larson for gladly taking the ball and running with it to the finish line. Thanks for the photos from Chris Renshaw, Claudia Crawford, Nandini Avery, Rodney Huff, and Fred Rozumalski. Thanks to Michael Gormley, Ashwani Dhiman, and Susan and Howard Judt for the lecture movies and recordings.For the 2nd edition, Mary Bowman-Cline quckly offered her beautiful artwork.

Most of all, thanks to Nikki for her endless hours of editing and formatting, boundless ideas, and inspiration.

# SRIVERM

*Swami Rama Institute of Vocational Education and Research
Malethi, Uttaranchal, India*

SRIVERM was established by the Trust in 2005 to give literacy, vocational, and socio-economic development to the underprivileged and underserved sections of the society in the hill district of Pauri Garhwal, Uttarkhand, deep in the Himalayas. Following are its current initiatives:

- Public School
- Vocational Training
- Ayurvedic Herbal Plantation

The Public School is presently covering children up to 8th grade, with approximately 100 students (to be progressively increased every year through grade 12). The Vocational Wing provides Vocational Training Courses in Computer Operation and Programming. Electrical Work, Tailoring and Sewing, and Plumbing. All graduates of the vocational program receive a National Council of Vocational Training (NCVT) certification. The Ayurvedic Herbal Plantation initiative provides education and training to the community in the cultivation of globally marketable herbal plants and their processing, as well as income - generation for the SRIVERM.

SRIVERM is located in the Pauri Garhwal Himalayas, via Kotdwar, Landsdowne, and Satpuli approximately (via car) 6 hours from Rishikesh and 7 hours from New Delhi. Please contact us for more information on how to: arrange a stay at the school guest house, volunteer for projects at the school or the Ayurvedic herbal gardens, or sponsor students and faculty.

To make a donation or for further information, please contact:

SRIVERM, INC.
2410 N. Farwell Avenue
Milwaukee, Wisconsin 53221
USA

Phone in the U.S.: (414) 273-1621

Email: info@theyogasociety.com

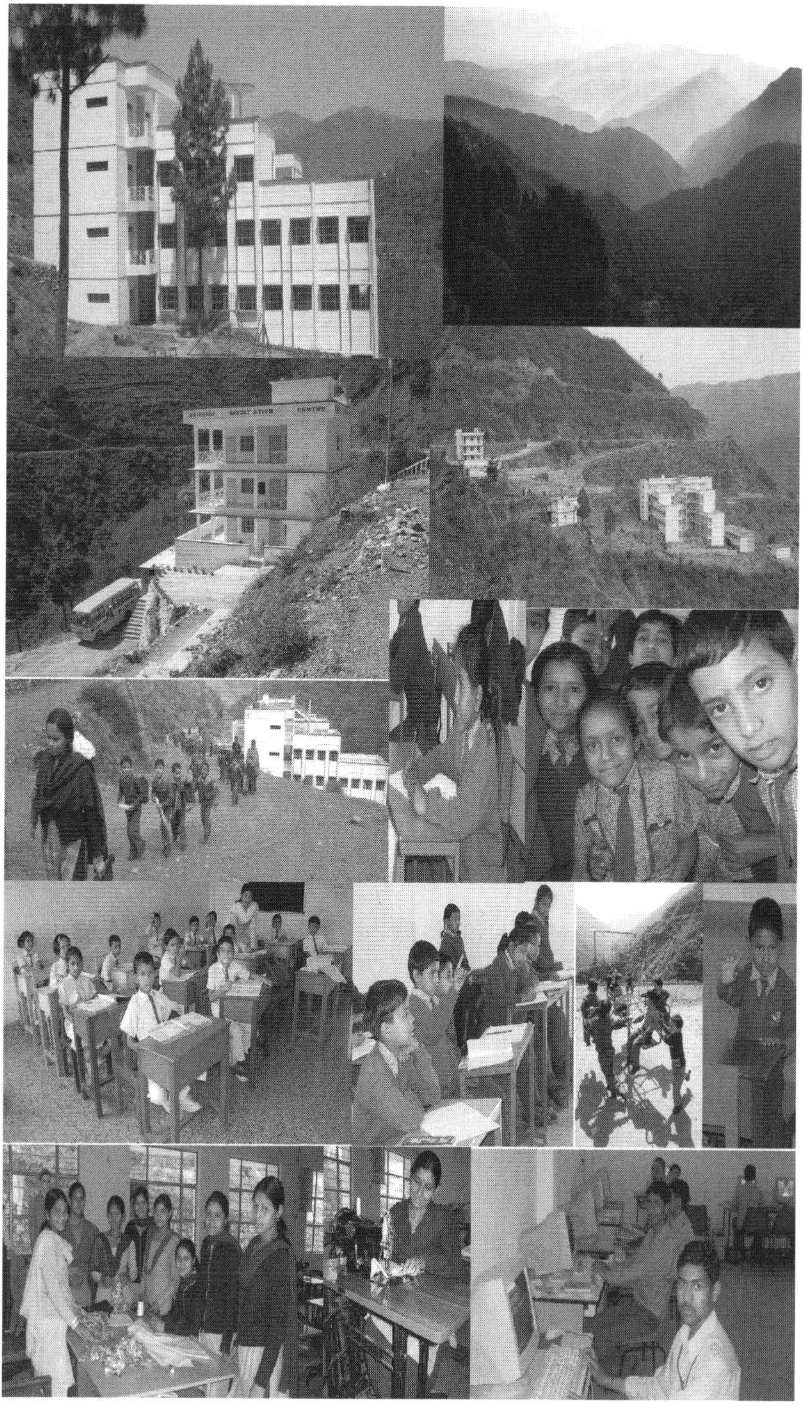

Printed in Great Britain
by Amazon.co.uk, Ltd.,
Marston Gate.